Ite, Missa Est.

I can only count
On my daily rosary
Prayers for company.

- T K Torme

Ite, Missa Est.

Also by T K Torme

Bull

In Conversation Vol 1

In Conversation Vol 2

In Conversation Vol 3

ITE MISSA EST
VOLUME 1

by

T. K. Torme

Silver Bow Publishing
720 Sixth Street, Unit # 5
New Westminster, BC CANADA

Title : Ite, Missa Est
Author: T K Torme
Cover Art : 'On the Waves' painting by Candice James
Layout & Design: Candice James
Editing: Candice James

All rights reserved including the right to reproduce or translate this book or any portions thereof, in any form without the permission of the publisher. Except for the use of short passages for review purposes, no part of this book may be reproduced, in part or in whole, or transmitted in any form or by any means, either by means electronically or mechanically, including photocopying, recording, or any information or storage retrieval system without prior permission in writing from the publisher or a licence from the Canadian Copyright Collective Agency (Access Copyright).

www.silverbowpublishing.com
info@silverbowpublishing.com
ISBN: 9781774031896 paperback
ISBN: 9781774031902 electronic book
© Silver Bow Publishing

Library and Archives Canada Cataloguing in Publication

Title: Ite, missa est. Volume 1 / by T.K. Torme.
Names: Torme, T. K., 1977- author.
Description: Poems.
Identifiers: Canadiana (print) 20210381655 | Canadiana (ebook) 20210381698 | ISBN 9781774031896
   (softcover) | ISBN 9781774031902 (EPUB)
Classification: LCC PS8639.O79 I84 2022 | DDC C811/.6—dc23

Dedication:

This book of poems is dedicated to the following people:

His Holiness Pope Francis – the coolest Pope on the planet

Father Geddes & Father Oballo @ Holy Family Church, Vancouver, BC

St. Scholastica my patron saint who has helped me write my haiku poems. St. Scholastica, watch over me.

Mathew Palmer & Bernadette Bonner in honor of their wedding on Saturday August 7, 2021

Tall the parishioners who attend Holy Family Church in Vancouver, BC

To Candice James whose editing of my book made the words shine.

To Isabella Mori & Margo Lamont who have been super supportive of my writing.

Ite, Missa Est.

FOREWORD

T K Torme suffers from Asperger's Syndrome but she was not diagnosed for many years and subsequently she suffered a great deal of trauma being misunderstood in her younger formative years.

This book of 266 haiku poems is a poignant look into the deep and personal spirituality of the poet. The misunderstandings and feelings of exclusion T K experienced in her younger years continue to challenge her as an adult as she still struggles with Asperger's Syndrome. T K finds the rosary to be her best, and only friend when she is mired in loneliness and just wanting what everyone else wants: to be liked and included.

"Ite Missa Est" is a religious and spiritual book concentrating on the soothing closeness to God she feels when praying to the rosary. T K Torme uses her God given talents to express how a marginalized person is able to cope with the challenges they are faced with when they have a strong commitment to God and their religion. This commitment elevates her spirituality so she is able to face all challenges that come her way. The rosary is both elemental in and essential to T K's well being in life.

T K Torme, through her own personal lens, takes us into her spiritual world which is the world of a person that has Asperger's Syndrome, and is sometimes unable to communicate easily with the non Asperger's surroundings she finds herself often immersed in.

T K Torme is a good Catholic, a fine child of God, and this book is a lovely offering filled with grace she has given to the world.

I highly recommend this book to everyone so they may better understand people with Asperger's who are not born with the social skills or given the social opportunities to connect with people easily and many times end up being unnecessarily marginalized by society at large. They have much to offer and the better the world understands them the greater endowed the world will be.

~ Candice James, Poet Laureate Emerita,
New Westminster, BC CANADA

Ite, Missa Est.

1

Ite, Missa Est.
Go, the Mass is finished – come
Again next Sunday.

2

All during the Mass:
Sit, kneel, stand all while you pray:
Catholic Aerobics.

3

It is not a sin
To kill a silverfish 'cause
The Priest told me so.

4

The Lord be with you
Et Cum Spiritu Tuo.
And With Thy Spirit.

Ite, Missa Est.

5

Would you rather have
No God and no peace or this:
You know God. Know peace.

6

There is a saying
That Jesus didn't tap 'cause
He loved to play Jazz.

7

Humility; Grace
Brings you riches and rewards
Sent from God above

8

The power of prayer:
Get rid of unwanted thoughts
Take away your sins.

9

Pray the Rosary
God's words are upon the beads
Directing your soul.

10

Pray the Rosary
The words will help calm you down
The Rosary rules.

11

While I am at Mass
All that sitting and kneeling
Daily exercise.

12

God is an ointment
Itches when you put it on
Heals – makes yourself whole.

13

Just say Hail Mary
Three times twice a day that will
Change your life around.

14

A scapular will
Protect you from all evil
Threats in this here world.

15

Let us all pray the
Rosary every day
Get in God's graces.

16

Decade Rosary
Best way to say Hail Mary
Pray them every day.

Ite, Missa Est.

17

I keep my decade
Rosary with me always
Protects me from harm.

18

The Rosary rules
The words will help calm you down
Pray the Rosary.

19

Pray them every day
Decade Rosary best way
To say Hail Mary.

20

Bright pink Rosary
All the prayers upon the beads
Holy Eucharist.

21

God is always there
When you pray the Rosary
Gives you good graces.

22

Answers all your prayers
When you pray the Rosary
Whispers in your heart.

23

Ten beads followed by
One for all those Hail Mary's
On the Rosary.

24

On the Rosary
Lie all of the mysteries
Gets you close to God.

Ite, Missa Est.

25

Always mean your prayers
When you say the Rosary
Mary will be pleased.

26

Pray the Rosary
Helps with your anxiety
Completely drug free.

27

What's a Rosary?
A great way to say your prayers
Every single day.

28

All my Rosaries
That I use to pray daily
Rest in my God Box.

29

Pray the Rosary:
Your life will start to change round
Blessings will abound.

30

God gives graces to
All who pray the Rosary
Every single day.

31

God blesses those who
Always say their daily prayers
The Rosary too.

32

The rosary rules
The words will help calm you down
Pray the rosary.

33

God's words are upon
The beads directing your soul
Pray the rosary.

34

Pray them every day
Decade rosary best way
To say Hail Mary.

35

Protects me from harm
With me always I keep my
Decade rosary.

36

Bright pink rosary
All the prayers upon the beads
Holy Eucharist.

37

God is always there
When you pray the rosary
Gives you good graces.

38

Answers all your prayers
When you pray the rosary
Whispers in your heart.

39

Ten beads followed by
One for all those Hail Mary's
On the Rosary.

40

On the rosary
Lie all of the mysteries
Gets you close to God.

41

Always mean your prayers
When you say the rosary
Mary will be pleased

42

Pray the rosary
Helps with your anxiety
Completely drug free.

43

What's a rosary?
A great way to say your prayers
Every single day.

44

All my rosaries
That I use to pray daily
Rest in my God Box.

45

Pray the Rosary:
Your life will start to change round
Blessings will abound.

46

God gives graces to
All who pray the rosary
Every single day.

47

God blesses those who
Always say their daily prayers
The rosary too.

48

Pray the rosary
Always faithfully daily
It will change your life.

49

This is my God Box:
All my rosaries lie here
For my daily prayer.

50

Bring my rosary
Every single place I go:
A portable prayer.

51

Pocketful of prayers
Always in my purse with me:
Holy Rosary.

52

God does speak to me
Every day when I pray the
Holy Rosary.

53

True manhood really
Is not macho but praying:
Holy Rosary.

54

A rosary in
My purse every single day
Keeps me safe from harm.

55

Just what is true strength?
Pray the rosary always:
Makes you gentle, wise.

56

If you do pray the
Rosary every day you
Gain true inner strength.

57

True inner strength comes
When you pray the rosary
Every single day.

58

Holy Rosary:
Meditate upon the beads:
Soothing for the soul.

59

A man who prays the
Rosary each day is a
True sign of manhood.

60

True strength always comes
In praying the rosary
Nct in lifting weights.

61

God's words are upon
The beads directing your soul
Pray the Rosary.

62

Protects me from harm
With me always I keep my
Decade Rosary.

63

For all Catholics
Father, Son and Holy Ghost
The Sign Of The Cross.

64

In the morning say,
O my God, I offer my
Heart and soul to you.

65

Orange rosary
Brightly colored string of beads
Pray them every day.

66

God is there for me
There on every single bead
Of the rosary.

67

A nun's rosary
Touched by Holy fingers: God
Whispers on the beads.

68

A Scapular will
Protect you from any harm
Wear it all the time.

69

The best defense tool
Is the mighty rosary
Pray it every day.

70

A rosary will
Help to calm your busy mind
To keep you focused.

71

A cold rosary
Can be pure hell to pray on:
A penance from God.

72

A rosary can
Quieten the story mind
Prepare for battle.

73

The Sign Of The Cross:
Say it every single day.
God will protect you.

74

Daily prayer routine
Along with my rosary
Keeps me close to God.

75

Daily rosary
Better than medications
Helps you sleep the night.

76

I always keep a
Rosary with me - for my
Spontaneous prayers.

Ite, Missa Est.

77

For anxiety
Pray the rosary daily
Really calms you down.

78

God calls to me when
I pray my rosary – my
Fingers on the beads.

79

Between my fingers
Lay my rosary that I
Always pray daily.

80

Good morning, Jesus:
Say this every single day –
It will change your life.

Ite, Missa Est.

81

God whispers in my
Ear: Pray the rosary for
Your daily blessings.

82

To be Catholic:
True faith and the rosary –
THE COMPLETE BIBLE.

83

Sweet heart of Mary,
Be my salvation. My God,
I love you. Save me.

84

Holy Eucharist:
Slowly dissolves on the tongue
God seeps in your soul.

85

To be Catholic:
Holy Eucharist on tongue;
Daily Rosary.

86

A true man will pray
The Rosary every day
Protect his woman.

87

A true woman will
Cover her head during Mass
In God's Holy House.

88

Be careful with words -
Never take Lord's name in vain:
Keep your language pure.

89

A real man eats meat;
Goes to Mass every Sunday:
Prays the rosary.

90

Always during Mass:
Holy Eucharist on tongue:
Weekly homily.

91

To be Catholic
Means praying the Rosary
And going to Mass.

92

After I pray the
Rosary; I fall asleep:
Calm and peaceful rest.

93

Inside my God Box
Lie all of my Rosaries
For my daily prayer.

94

A Hail Mary goes
A long way throughout the day:
Quick prayer on the go.

95

Pray the Rosary
Every single day to fight
Your daily anger.

96

To get rid of your
Daily anger every day
Pray the Rosary.

97

just cannot fit
All of my Rosaries in
My tiny God Box.

98

Just a rosary
Prayer every day will help you
Be closer to God.

99

Every Sunday at
Mass the Rosary is prayed:
God in every heart.

100

I love rosaries:
Hail Marys upon the beads -
Soothing to the soul.

Ite, Missa Est.

101

Priests who yells at you
To study your faith - I have
Great respect for them.

102

Pray the Rosary
Every single day and you
Will always be blessed.

103

Father, forgive them.
Why Hast Tou Forsaken Me?
Commend My Spirit.

104

I did not pray my
Morning decade rosary
Every day last week.

105

Unless I tell you
I confess via Haiku
You will never know.

106

I spend time alone
Just praying the rosary
Every single day.

107

When I do not pray
The rosary every day
I just cannot sleep.

108

The Sign Of The Cross:
Father, Son, and Holy Ghost:
Holy Trinity.

109

I would rather pray

A Hail Mary every day

Than to get angry.

110

A rosary will

Really help to calm you down

Lowers blood pressure.

111

When I do not pray

The rosary every day

I become anxious.

112

I love to go to

Confession every Sunday

Highlight of my week.

113

Father, would you please
Bless my rosary for me?
I'd really like that.

114

Pax Domini Sit
Semper Vobis Cum Et Cum
Spiritu Tuo.

115

I am Catholic
I go to the Latin Mass
Pray the rosary.

116

The line up today
Was way too long for me to
Go to confession.

117

I cannot resist
Buying books and rosaries
At Holy Family.

118

Father Oballo,
Would you please touch and bless my
Brand new rosary?

119

Inside my God Box
Rest all of my rosaries
I use for my prayers.

120

Be Thee, God Father
Almighty, in unity
Of the Holy Ghost.

121

As a Catholic
I have lots of rosaries
For my daily prayer.

122

Mini rosary:
Perfect way to say your prayers
Every single day.

123

Nestled in my hand
Lies my mini rosary
A portable prayer.

124

A portable prayer
In my mini rosary
Nestled in my hand.

125

My rosary gives
Me comfort, dries all my tears
Keeps me company.

126

In my lonliness,
My rosary is really
My one, only friend.

126

Many Catholics
Own a lot of rosaries
For their daily prayer.

127

I can only count
On my daily rosary
Prayers for company.

128

A rosary is
The perfect Valentine's gift
For a Catholic girl.

129

My God Box is packed
Full of all the rosaries
I have collected.

130

I love to pray my
Rosary every single
Day. It keeps me calm.

131

If more people prayed
The rosary there would be
Less anxiety.

Ite, Missa Est.

132

I would rather pray
My rosary than become
Angry at people.

133

In the summer time
My rosary gives me prayers
Every single day.

134

Every single day
My rosary gives me prayers
In the summer time.

135

The only solace
I have is my rosary
No other comfort.

136

Through Whom, O Lord, Thou

Create, hallow, quicken, bless

And give them to us.

137

God does reward those

Who do pray the rosary

Every single day.

138

Many Catholics

Do keep a car rosary

For their daily prayers.

139

Quick Sign Of The Cross

Keeps all evil things away -

And Satan at bay.

140

My life in God's hands
He directs me in my life
Life and death balance.

141

Holy Eucharist
Memories of a distant past
God's House - a ghost town.

142

Fresh Priest on the job
7 a.m. confessions
At Holy Family.

143

Early confessions
Fresh Priest at Holy Family
In the crying room.

Ite, Missa Est.

144

God is now online
Public Masses have been banned
Communities divide.

145

Where church pews were full
Now just a silent echo
God's House: A ghost town.

146

God's house once was full
Now a shadow of itself
As ghosts walk the halls.

148

A true man is one
Who will pray the rosary
Every single day.

149

To confess early
Wash away all of my sins
Clean for the whole day.

150

Ite Ad Joseph
Go to Joseph for all things
He will keep you pure.

151

Would you rather have
No God and no peace or this:
You know God. Know peace.

OEM 152

To pray the Rosary
God's words are upon the beads
Directing your soul.

153

Pray the Rosary
The words will help calm you down
The Rosary rules.

154

While I am at Mass
All that sitting and kneeling
Daily exercise.

155

Ite, Missa Est.
Go, the Mass is finished – come
Again next Sunday.

156

Can I use Haiku
Poems to confess all of
My grave sins to God?

157

Always watch over
Me or I will betray You
Just like Judas did.

158

Pray the rosary
Always faithfully daily
It will change your life.

159

Let us all pray the
Rosary every day
Get in God's graces.

160

Decade Rosary
Best way to say Hail Mary
Pray them every day.

161

I keep my decade
Rosary with me always
Protects me from harm.

162

The Rosary rules
The words will help calm you down
Pray the Rosary.

163

God's words are upon
The beads directing your soul
Pray the Rosary.

164

Pray them every day
Decade Rosary best way
To say Hail Mary.

165

Bright pink Rosary
All the prayers upon the beads
Holy Eucharist.

166

Answers all your prayers
When you pray the Rosary
Whispers in your heart.

167

Ten beads followed by
One for all those Hail Mary's
On the Rosary.

168

Always mean your prayers
When you say the Rosary
Mary will be pleased.

169

Pray the Rosary
Helps with your anxiety
Completely drug free.

170

What's a Rosary?
A great way to say your prayers
Every single day.

171

All my Rosaries
That I use to pray daily
Rest in my God Box.

172

Pray the Rosary:
Your life will start to change round
Blessings will abound.

173

God gives graces to
All who pray the Rosary
Every single day.

174

God blesses those who
Always say their daily prayers
The Rosary too.

175

The rosary rules
The words will help calm you down
Pray the rosary.

176

God's words are upon
The beads directing your soul
Pray the rosary.

177

Pray them every day
Decade rosary best way
To say Hail Mary.

178

Protects me from harm
With me always I keep my
Decade rosary.

179

Bright pink rosary
All the prayers upon the beads
Holy Eucharist.

180

God is always there
When you pray the rosary
Gives you good graces.

181

Answers all your prayers
When you pray the rosary
Whispers in your heart.

182

Ten beads followed by
One for all those Hail Mary's
On the Rosary.

183

On the rosary
Lie all of the mysteries
Gets you close to God.

184

Always mean your prayers
When you say the rosary
Mary will be pleased

185

Pray the rosary
Helps with your anxiety
Completely drug free.

186

What's a rosary?
A great way to say your prayers
Every single day.

187

All my rosaries
That I use to pray daily
Rest in my God Box.

188

Pray the Rosary:
Your life will start to change round
Blessings will abound.

189

God gives graces to
All who pray the rosary
Every single day.

190

God blesses those who
Always say their daily prayers
The rosary too.

191

This is my God Box:
All my rosaries lie here
For my daily prayer.

192

Bring my rosary
Every single place I go:
A portable prayer.

Ite, Missa Est.

193

Pocketful of prayers
Always in my purse with me:
Holy Rosary.

194

God does speak to me
Every day when I pray the
Holy Rosary.

195

True manhood really
Is not macho but praying:
Holy Rosary.

196

A rosary in
My purse every single day
Keeps me safe from harm.

197

Just what is true strength?
Pray the rosary always:
Makes you gentle, wise.

198

If you do pray the
Rosary every day you
Gain true inner strength.

199

True inner strength comes
When you pray the rosary
Every single day.

200

Holy Rosary:
Meditate upon the beads:
Soothing for the soul.

201

A man who prays the
Rosary every day is
True sign of manhood.

202

True strength always comes
In praying the rosary
Not in lifting weights.

203

God is there for me
On every singular bead
Of the rosary.

204

Orange rosary
Brightly colored string of beads
Pray them every day.

205

A nun's rosary
Touched by Holy fingers: God
Whispers on the beads.

206

A rosary can
Quieten the story mind
Prepare for battle.

207

The best defense tool
Is the mighty rosary
Pray it every day.

208

A rosary will
Help to calm your busy mind
To keep you focused.

209

A cold rosary
Can be pure hell to pray on:
A penance from God.

210

Daily prayer routine
Along with my rosary
Keeps me close to God.

211

Daily rosary
Better than medications
Helps you sleep the night.

212

always keep a
Rosary with me - for my
Spontaneous prayers.

213

For anxiety
Pray the rosary daily
Really calms you down.

214

God calls to me when
I pray my rosary – my
Fingers on the beads.

215

Between my fingers
Lay my rosary that I
Always pray daily.

216

I can only count
On my daily rosary
Prayers for company.

Ite, Missa Est.

217

God whispers in my
Ear: Pray the rosary for
Your daily blessings.

218

Always during Mass:
S t, kneel, stand all while you pray:
Catholic Aerobics.

219

To be Catholic:
Holy Eucharist on tongue;
Daily Rosary.

220

A true man will pray
The Rosary every day
Protect his woman.

221

A real man eats meat;
Goes to Mass every Sunday:
Prays the rosary.

222

Blessings all around:
Masked, invisibility -
On the rosary.

223

To be Catholic
Means praying the Rosary
And going to Mass.

224

After I pray the
Rosary; I fall asleep:
Calm and peaceful rest.

225

It is not a sin
To kill a silverfish 'cause
The Priest told me so.

226

Inside my God Box
Lie all of my Rosaries
For my daily prayer.

227

Pray the Rosary
Every single day to fight
Your daily anger.

228

To get rid of your
Daily anger every day
Pray the Rosary.

229

I just cannot fit
All of my Rosaries in
My tiny God Box.

230

Just a rosary
Prayer every day will help you
Be closer to God.

231

Every Sunday at
Mass the Rosary is prayed:
God in every heart.

232

I love rosaries:
Hail Marys upon the beads -
Soothing to the soul.

233

Pray the Rosary
Every single day and you
Will always be blessed.

234

The Lord be with you
Et Cum Spiritu Tuo.
And With Thy Spirit.

235

I did not pray my
Morning decade rosary
Every day last week.

236

I spend time alone
Just praying the rosary
Every single day.

237

When I do not pray

The rosary every day

I just cannot sleep.

238

A rosary will

Really help to calm you down

Lowers blood pressure.

239

When I do not pray

The rosary every day

I become anxious.

240

Father, would you please

Bless my rosary for me?

I'd really like that.

241

Pax Domini Sit
Semper Vobis Cum Et Cum
Spiritu Tuo.

242

I am Catholic
I go to the Latin Mass
Pray the rosary.

243

The line up today
Was way too long for me to
Go to confession.

244

I cannot resist
Buying books and rosaries
At Holy Family.

245

Father Oballo,
Would you please touch and bless my
Brand new rosary?

246

Inside my God Box
Rest all of my rosaries
That I use to pray.

247

As a Catholic
I have lots of rosaries
For my daily prayer.

248

Mini rosary:
Perfect way to say your prayers
Every single day.

Ite, Missa Est.

249

Nestled in my hand
Lies my mini rosary
A portable prayer.

250

A portable prayer
Lies my mini rosary
Nestled in my hand.

251

My rosary gives
Me comfort, dries all my tears
Keeps me company.

252

In my lonliness,
My rosary is really
My one, only friend.

253

Many Catholics
Own a lot of rosaries
For their daily prayer.

254

I can only count
On my daily rosary
Prayers for company.

255

A rosary is
The perfect Valentine's gift
For a Catholic girl.

256

My God Box is packed
Full of all the rosaries
I have collected.

257

I love to pray my
Rosary every single
Day. It keeps me calm.

258

If more people prayed
The rosary there would be
Less anxiety.

259

I would rather pray
My rosary than become
Angry at people.

260

In the summer time
My rosary gives me prayers
Every single day.

261

At seven a.m.
Is the best time to confess
The Priest's really fresh.

262

It has been so long
Seems I've forgotten how to
Pray the rosary.

263

A rosary prayer
Is a really good way to
Always talk to God.

264

My rosary keeps
Me calm when I say my prayers
Every single day.

265

When I am to die,
I would like to be buried
With my rosary.

266

What better way to
Start the day than drink coffee
And pray rosary?

www.ingramcontent.com/pod-product-compliance
Lightning Source LLC
Chambersburg PA
CBHW062152100526
44589CB00014B/1808